JOHN AND HIS FRIENDS

THIS IS a story about a boy named John. He lives in the middle of the block. He has a mother and a father and three brothers and two sisters, and a dog and a cat and two rabbits.

JOHN GIVES right-away obedience. When Mother calls he says, "All right, Mother." John loves Mary, the Blessed Mother of Jesus. He wants to be like her.

Can a boy be like Our Blessed Mother? Of course he can.

JOHN PAYS attention in school. He studies his lessons. He is doing what God wants. He said something to God before he started to study. Guess what it was.

He said, "I will do what God wants."

JOHN plays fair with his brothers and sisters and his friends. He waits his turn, and he shares his toys, and he does not fight or quarrel.

THIS GIRL and this boy live next door to John. They are John's friends. I don't know their names. Are they doing what God wants?

JOHN AND his brothers and sisters run to meet their Dad. God wants us to be nice to our mothers and fathers.

JOHN TALKS to God often during the day. He stops in to visit Jesus in church. He prays: “Jesus, I love You. I will try to do what You want, always. Please help me.”

The rest of the story will be in your next Treasure Box.

MARIA

Maria was a very happy girl. But when she got up one morning, she was feeling *very* cross. She frowned.

Then she brushed her teeth and washed her face.

She put on her dress.

She put on her socks and shoes.

Mr. Parakeet said, "Maria, where is my food? I want my breakfast!"

Mr. Parakeet yelled, "I need clean water."

Maria walked right by Mr. Parakeet.

She turned her head away from him.

She was really a very cross little girl.

Maria walked into the garden.

The sun was shining.

She saw a mother robin feeding a baby robin.

She saw a mother cat washing a kitten's face.

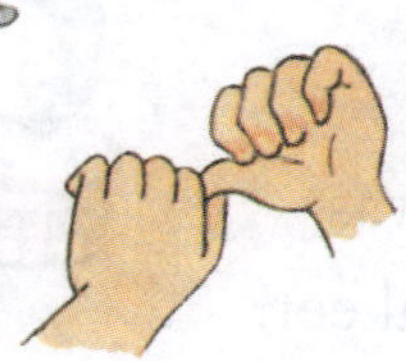

She saw a puppy playing with a ball.

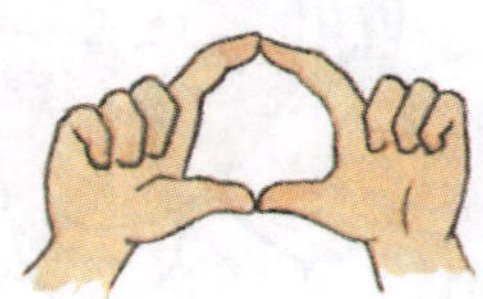

Everyone in the garden was happy. The sun seemed to be smiling.

Maria wondered what to do with her frown.

She wiped it off her face.

And threw it into a rose bush.

She ran back into the house.

And danced around Mr. Parakeet.

She filled his water cup.

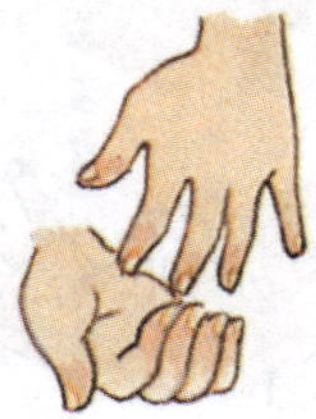

She filled his seed cup overflowing.

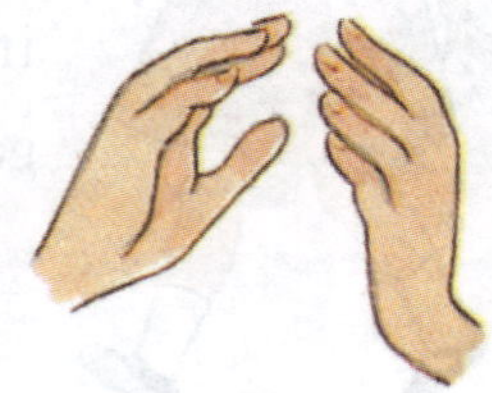

Maria was happy again,

and so was Mr. Parakeet.

SUNNY'S CURIOSITY

Father George's motorcycle broke down three miles from Matongu. He could not mend it, and the Angels did not help at all. In fact, one of them said, "It's Father George's own fault for not bringing a spare piece of string."

Luckily, several big strong men had come over from Matongu to meet the missioner, so they just put the motorcycle on some big sticks and carried it to the village. Everyone came out to meet Father George.

Ntaka-Ntaka, Sunny's mother, was one of the first to greet the missioner. How pleased she was that he had come! Sunny was there, too. He did not want to miss a thing. Wupsy was keeping an eye on him, because he was never sure what Sunny might do next. Wupsy was sorry that Sunny did not realize how wonderful it was to have Father George come at last to Matongu. Although Sunny had been baptized, he had not been taught anything about God.

The spot for the new mission was on a little hill just outside the village. There was room for a church and a house for the missioners. Big trees stretched out their branches and gave shade. There was a place for a fine garden, too. In it, Father could grow banana trees, and beans, and manioc (which is a kind of potato) and other things that people eat in Africa. And there was a little dancing stream to water the garden. At the bottom of the hill, the forest began.

Father George brought lots of boxes with him for the new mission. When they had all been carried to the top of the hill and the motorcycle was put down beside them very carefully, Father George honked the horn as loud as he could. Everyone heard the horn and came out of their huts to see what was going on.

Father George said, "We have come to Matongu to teach all of you about God. We will also take care of you when you are sick, and teach the children how to read and write."

Then he asked for ten strong men who would like to help him build a hut to sleep in. Everybody wanted to help, and he sent them off into the forest to cut down branches and tall grasses. The men who had carried Father George's boxes through the forest to Matongu were resting and telling everyone all about the huge lion they had chased away. Then they helped too.

Sunny was wearing new clothes that his mother had made for him for this special day. He was near Father George, watching him open the cases. From one box Father George took a big tent, which the men put up. Another box was full of hammers and saws and other tools. Another had all the things needed for Mass, while a fourth was full of little bottles and boxes, all carefully labeled.

A young friend of Sunny's, called Ngomi, was specially interested in this box, and when Father George was looking the other way, he snatched a bottle and ran off with it.

Sunny thought it was a good idea, so he snatched one too. Wupsy tried to stop him, but Sunny would not listen. He tucked the bottle inside his shirt and said, "Ngomi, wait for me!"

Then Father George noticed the box was open and closed it quickly.

"Imagine being naughty like that even when there aren't any devils around!" Wupsy said to himself as he flew anxiously after Ngomi and Sunny. There was nothing very bad in the bottles, but he knew the boys must not swallow too much of either one.

The two boys sat down in the shade and looked at the bottles. Then they opened them to see what was inside. Sunny tasted one of the pink pills that he found in his bottle.

"Mmm! It's good . . . have some!" he said, and he gave his friend Ngomi three of them. Then he had some more himself.

Ngomi tasted the brown sticky stuff that was in his bottle. It tasted awful, so he threw it away. Sunny decided to let one of the pills melt in his mouth instead of swallowing it whole. It tasted so bitter inside that he threw the rest of them away.

Wupsy was sitting nearby, trying to get Sunny to stop and think about what he had done, but Sunny was too busy to listen.

Sunny and Ngomi decided that they would play a game of hide and seek at the edge of the forest.

Pretty soon Sunny sat down on a tree trunk and started rubbing his tummy. At first Ngomi laughed at him. But pretty soon both boys were crying–very softly at first, then louder and louder till even the birds were frightened and flew away.

Just then Ntaka-Ntaka, who was looking for Sunny, came along the path. She found both boys crying and saying, "I have a fire inside my tummy."

Wupsy flew down and whispered to Ntaka-Ntaka, "Remember when Sunny had fire outside and Father George cured him? Surely he can cure the fire inside, too. You'd better take the two little boys to him right away."

Ntaka-Ntaka picked up the little boys, tucked one under each arm, and set off to see Father George.

She found him looking over his medicine bottles and wondering what had happened to two of them. As soon as he saw Sunny and Ngomi he asked, "What have they been eating?"

"O-o-o-o-h, Father," they moaned. And between floods of tears they told him the whole story. The boys were really sorry they had been so naughty.

Father George was not cross with Sunny and Ngomi. In fact, he said the boys were lucky they had taken *those* bottles and not others that could have made them feel even worse. Then he gave them each another kind of pill and sent them home to bed.

The next morning the two little boys woke up to find that the pains had gone, and before the day was over they were running around as usual.

Neither of them ever went near Father George's boxes again.

AT THE SEA-SIDE

When I was down beside the sea
A wooden spade they gave to me
  To dig the sandy shore.
My holes were empty like a cup.
In every hole the sea came up,
  Till it could come no more.

—Robert Louis Stevenson

how would you play If you had no games or toys or books

Sometimes when we played outside without toys, we played *Building a House*. If there was a sandy place, it was very simple. All we had to do was trace our lines on the ground with a stick. But if it was a place with cement or pavement, we needed a piece of chalk, or a little piece of plaster, to draw our lines on the ground. We each designed our own house, with rooms and doors and windows. You know, just the way real architects make their drawings when they plan a house. The drawing had to be big, so that we could walk in and out of the house and visit each other. Of course, nobody was allowed to walk through the walls or windows! Sometimes it was fun to put in long staircases, even winding ones, on which we had to walk with very small steps.

When we knew all about our own house and our neighbor's house, we would play the game of the Impolite Visitor. One player would sit in his house, while the Visitor pretended to ring the doorbell. He would then lead him in and show him around, just as if he was really showing a guest his new house. They had a lovely conversation. But at any unexpected moment the Visitor would call: "My dinner is burning!" or "Oh, I forgot my handbag!" or any silly excuse, and dash away. The owner of the house had to try and catch him before he reached the front door. If there were more than two players, the others would watch that they did not step anywhere they were not supposed to. If someone stepped in the wrong place, he would be the loser.

The Story of Gold Chick

Once there was a little hen named Gold-Chick. She was called Gold-Chick because every day she laid a little golden egg. You can easily see that she was a very special little hen, and you will believe me if I tell you that many people would have loved to own her. But the little hen belonged to herself and lived all alone. People might try–but they could not catch or buy her.

There also lived three women who happened to hear about this special little hen. Of course, they very much wanted to own her.

"If I could catch that hen," said the first woman, "I would keep her in a golden cage and keep the golden eggs all for myself. I would be the richest woman alive."

The following day she took a net and a small bag full of sweet corn and went to the place where the hen lived. There she spread the net on the ground, with a string attached so that she could pull it right over the little hen. Then she scattered the corn and hid in the bushes.

"Little Gold-Chick, come out, I want to talk to you!" she called in her sweetest voice.

The hen came and asked, "What do you want of me?"

"I have heard that you live all alone," she answered, "so I have come to spread a tasty meal for you."

"I do not care for your sweet corn!" replied the clever little hen. "You can take it home

again. And take your net right along with it, for you will never catch a special little hen like me."

The woman went home. When she told the others how she had fared, the second woman said to herself:

"*I* will be more clever when *I* go tomorrow. *I* will talk the little hen into coming with *me*."

When she came to the place where the hen lived, she called, "Little hen, come out, I want to talk to you!"

"What do you want?" asked the little hen from behind the bushes.

"Little hen, I have heard so much about your beauty and your lovely voice," cooed the woman. "I think it a shame that you should live where nobody sees you. Come with me, and I will give you a house of marble to live in. I will give parties in your honor. All the important people in town will be your friends. Your story will be in the newspapers, and you will become the most famous hen in the world."

"Go right home again!" said the little hen indignantly. "I do not care for fame and false friends. You can never bribe a special little hen like *me!*"

The woman went home and cried with anger because she had been so unsuccessful.

The third woman was poor and had a house full of hungry children.

"My house is not good enough for such a special hen," she thought, "but if I could get *just one* of those golden eggs, my children would not have to starve."

The next day she got up early and went to the place where the hen lived. The hen was standing there, and got very angry when she saw the woman.

"Go away and don't bother me!" she shouted. "You can *never* catch or bribe a special little hen like me."

"Well do I know that," answered the poor woman. "But for the sake of my hungry children, allow me one question. What can a lonely little hen do with so many golden eggs? If I had but *one* of them, I could buy food for my children. Please give me one of your precious little eggs for them."

The little hen flew onto the poor woman's shoulder and rubbed her head against the woman's cheek.

"I have lived alone here all my life," she cried. "Hundreds of people have come and tried to catch me or to bribe me because of my golden eggs, but in all these years nobody has ever *asked* me for them. Take me home with you, and I will lay a golden egg for your children every day. Only keep it a secret, for I want nothing better than to live simply and unknown like an ordinary little hen!"

And that is exactly what happened.